MASON
and Invincible Igor

By Robin Heald   Illustrated by Alexandra Artigas

SAPPHIRE FAMILY SERIES

Mason and Invincible Igor – Sapphire Family Series
By Robin Heald
Illustrated by Alexandra Artigas

Robin Ray Books
642 Liberty Street
Ashland, OR 97520
Phone: 541-944-3199
Email: robinheald@robinheald.com
Website: www.robinheald.com

Copyright © 2023 by Robin Heald

All rights reserved. No part of this publication may be reproduced by any means, stored in a retrieval system, or transmitted in whole or in part, in any form or by any means, electronic, mechanical, photocopying, recording, or otherwise without the express written consent of the publisher, except for the inclusion of brief quotations in a review.

ISBN (Print book): 978-1-7363557-4-9
ISBN (E-Book): 978-1-7363557-5-6

Library of Congress Control Number: 2023940891

First Edition. Printed in the United States of America

Book production by One On One Book Production and Marketing, West Hills, California.

To my students at Pomegranate,
for their imaginations and for inspiring me.
~ Robin

To my beloved Kola, Andrei and Sofia,
my sources of happiness and constant
inspiration.
~ Ale

ABOUT THE BOOK

Book 3 – ***Mason and Invincible Igor:*** Eight-year-old Mason writes and illustrates his own superhero series, *Invincible Igor*. Tonight his goal is to finish book six in the series. But with all the interruptions, how can he? His six-year-old sister, animal-loving Alicia, needs Mason's drawing and spelling skills to make a sign that will keep her "pooping machine" guinea pig safe. And now there is a racket coming from the bathroom, thanks to his youngest siblings – four-year-old twins, Jackson and Jillian. It's a big responsibility being the oldest kid in the family. Will Mason ever be able to finish his book? Or maybe something will happen that will inspire the ending.

Mason and Invincible Igor is written for read-aloud and for early readers. An art activity, and interactive questions to promote memory recall and emotional intelligence are included.

ABOUT THE SERIES

I was in my classroom when a student asked,
"I wonder what my sister is doing right now?"

The student's question made me think about a child's emerging concept of time; that of being aware of life happening elsewhere, outside of the child's own experience.

Each book in the **Sapphire Family Series** is told from a different point of view: that of the twins, Jackson and Jillian, their older sister, Alicia, and big brother, Mason.

All three books take place during the same period of time, early evening.

Although the books can stand alone, read together they offer a three-dimensional exploration of sibling interactions and family dynamics. Reading the story from different points of view is a first step in *thinking beyond oneself*.

Book 1 – ***Jackson and Jillian:*** Four-year-old twins, Jackson and Jillian, love pretending and love doing things all by themselves. But tonight, tooth-brushing will lead to a brush with disaster.

Book 2 – ***Alicia and Annie:*** Six-year-old Alicia wants to be a responsible pet owner. But now Annie, her new guinea pig, is missing.

My intention is that the **Sapphire Family Series** will offer children compelling characters with whom they can identify and grow, and present positive, realistic family dynamics that will delight them.

I hope you enjoy reading
Mason and Invincible Igor
and the other books in the series.

Robin Heald
Ashland, Oregon

Knock, knock! "Mason?"

Maybe if Mason didn't answer, his sister, Alicia, would go away.

Knock, knock, knock! "Mason Sapphire!"

"What?!"

Alicia opened the door. "Are you making another *Igor* book?" Alicia asked.

Yep, number six.

"Mason, would you please draw Annie?"

Mason read Alicia's sign.

Kep the Dor Closd

He quickly sketched Annie.

He also corrected his sister's spelling. She *was* only in first grade. Mason was eight and in third grade, and he loved spelling. This week's *super-brain third grade* spelling word was *scalawag*. It meant *rascal* or *imp*.

"Twinkle, twinkle, little brush. Hush and mush and slush and crush." Singing floated from the bathroom.

"Wrong words!" Screaming pierced the air.

Pok-pok-pok! Blum-blum blum! Something fell.

"See what you made me do!"

Jackson and Jillian! Mason's little brother and sister were the cause of the ruckus. Four-year-old twin scalawags!

16

At this rate, he'd never finish his Igor story.

Mason called for Mom.

"She's downstairs," said Alicia. "It's your turn to help the twins. I already rescued Annie from them."

Mason rushed past Alicia into the bathroom.

"Why was I born first?" he muttered.

"What fell? What's going on?" shouted Mason.

He froze. What was going on was *CHAOS*, last week's *super-brain* word. It meant out of control.

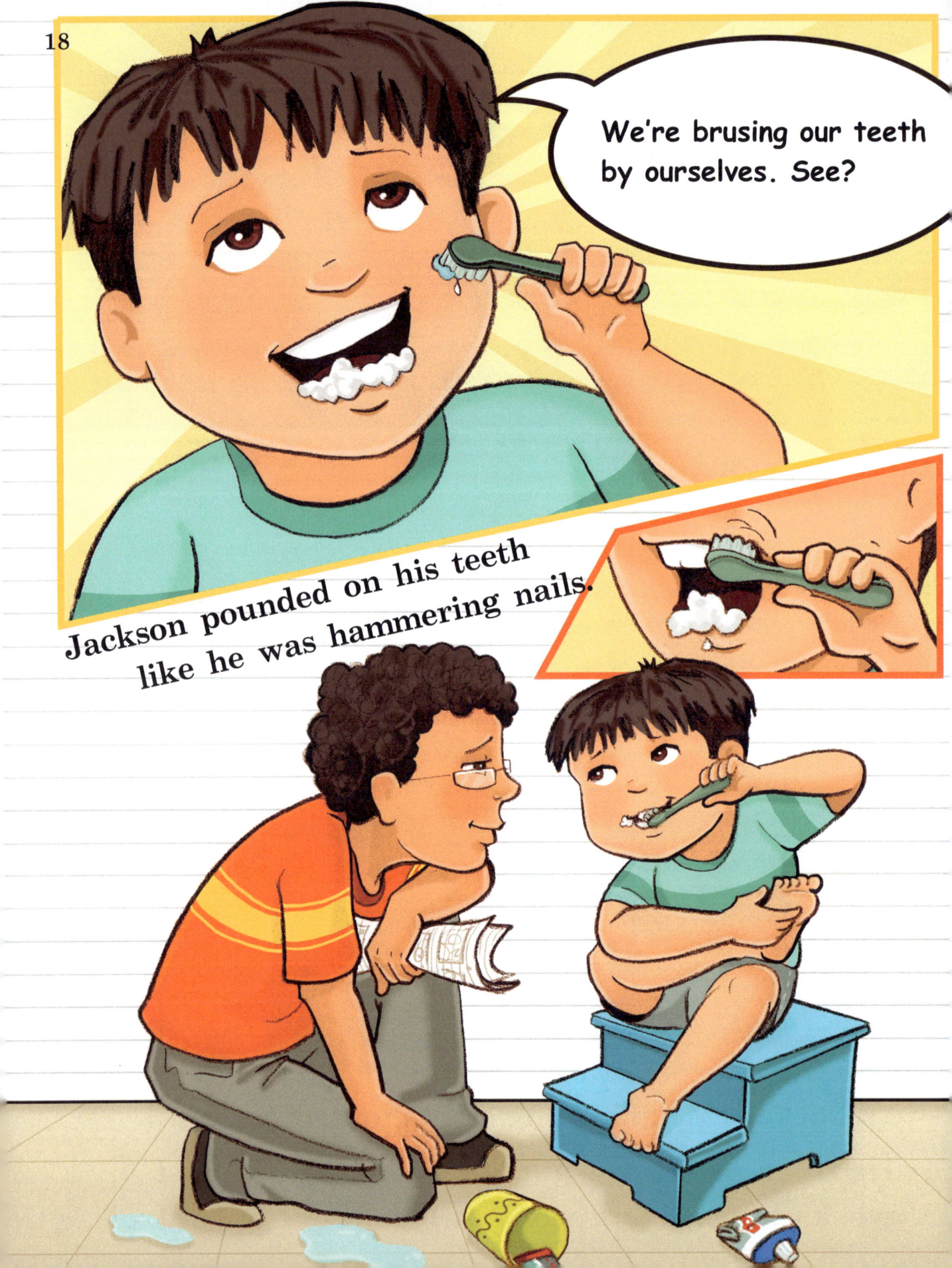

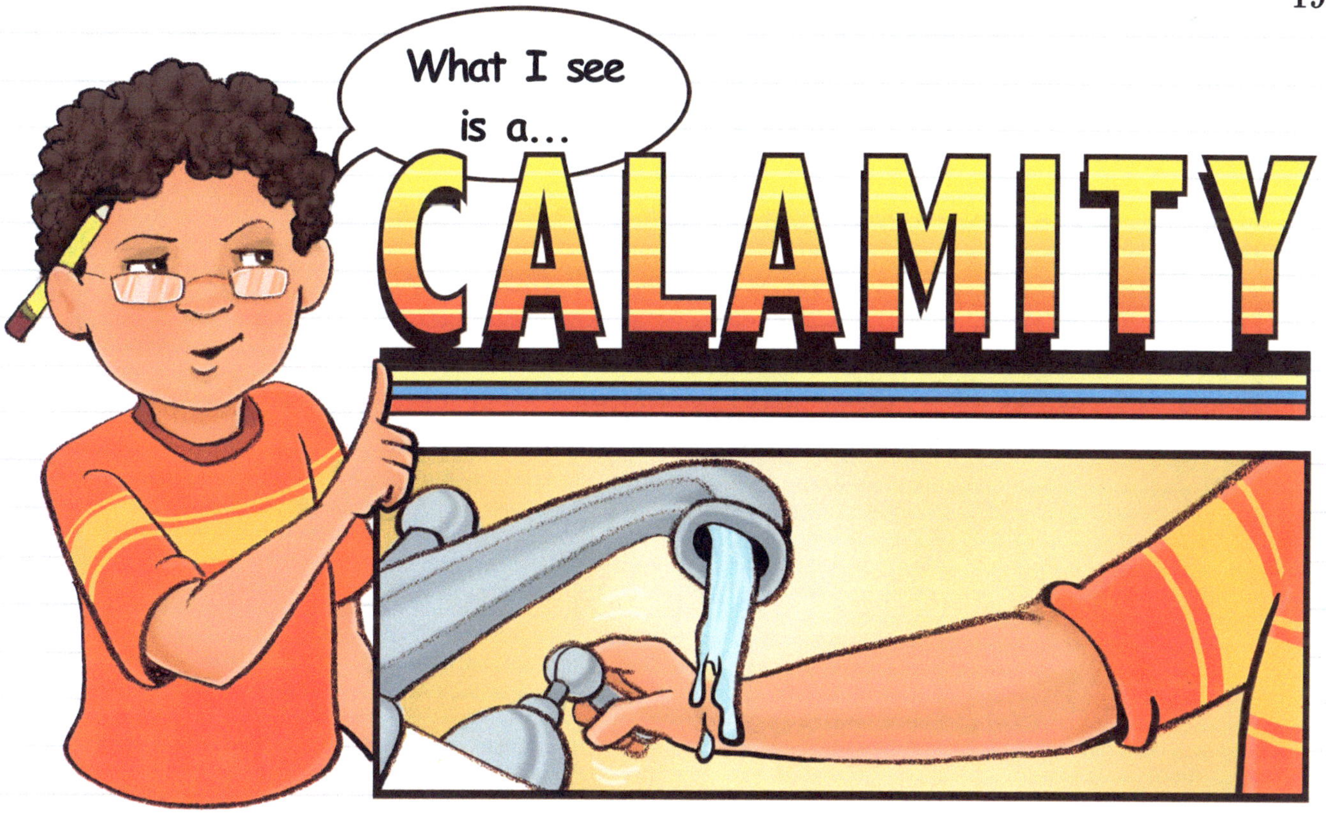

"What I see is a...

CALAMITY

"Don't waste water when you brush," Mason said. "Jackie, don't chew on the bristles."

"Woof!" Jackson barked. "I'm a dog, and the toothbrush is a bone." Mason made up a drawing in his head.

20

Mason had accidentally brought his *Igor* story into the bathroom.

Mason helped Jackson brush his teeth.

"Small circles around every single tooth: on top, in back and in front," said Mason. "Now you try."

Jackson stared at Mason like he was a superhero.

"You've made a new *Igor* story!" said Jillian.

Mason smiled. The twins knew every *Igor* story by heart. If he finished book six, maybe he'd read it to them at bedtime. He still had to finish his homework.

"We never ever slobber." Jillian dripped toothpaste foam. Another drawing popped into Mason's head.

Mason plucked his *Igor* pages from Jackson. "I'm going to finish my story. You guys need to wipe your mouths, and clean up this mess."

"You're not the boss of us!"

"You're not the boss, moss, hoss of us," Jackson rhymed.

"Hoss is not a word," Jillian shrieked.

"Yes it is," said Jackson. "Hosses eat hay."

Mason thought of a drawing to go with Jackson's joke.

Mason finished his homework. The assignment was to use two *super-brain third grade* words in one sentence.

The Sapphire scalawags created chaos in the bathroom. Cool!

Back to Igor. Igor was just about to save the soccer team from the falling tree.

What next?

Igor seizes the tree.
He's got to save the soccer team.

and grinds it into the ground.
The team cheers!

"HELLO! Anyone home?"
Dad was home from work.

Who wants ice cream?

Dad brought delectable desserts from his restaurant. Delectable was better than delicious.

Who wouldn't want ice cream?

Usually Mom and Dad didn't let him draw at the table. But Annie was on Alicia's lap. That wasn't allowed, either. The twins were stirring and slurping their bowls of ice cream.

Suddenly, Mason had an idea for an ending.

"Now we have to brush our teeth all over again," said Jackson.

Mason remembered when Dad would carry him and Alicia upstairs.

Sometimes he missed being a little kid. But being older meant he knew how to write and draw *Igor* stories.

Jackson's garbled voice echoed downstairs.

"Brush, brush, brush your teeth, circle round and round."

That's what Mason had taught them!

Mom and Alicia talked, while Mason drew and wrote.

"We want IGOR! We want IGOR!" the twins chanted from upstairs.

"Looks like you're the reader tonight... You're my superhero, Magnificent Mason."

"There! Done!" Mason grabbed his story and ran upstairs to Jackson and Jillian's room.

He imagined Igor flying behind him, cheering him on.

Mason read Jackson and Jillian all of book six.

The twins scooted closer to Mason as Igor seized the tree mid-air.

Mason said goodnight to the scalawags and flopped into bed.

Book six! The twins had distracted him, but they had also inspired him.

What would inspire book seven? Mason wondered.

Questions for memory recall:

1. What are some new words Mason has learned?
2. Why does Alicia knock on Mason's door?
3. How does Mason help Jackson and Jillian?
4. What kind of ice cream does Mason like?
5. What is Mason's *Igor* story about?

Questions to enrich emotional intelligence:

1. Mason loves making art. What do you love doing?
2. Do you think Mason likes being the oldest child? Why?
3. Why do you think Mason sometimes misses being little?
4. What special powers would your superhero have?
5. Would Mason be a good friend? Why?

MAKE YOUR OWN SUPERHERO

Copy this page and fill in the details of your own superhero.

Name: _____ Age: _____

Hometown or Planet: _____

Special Powers: _____

Robin Heald grew up in Philadelphia, but now lives in Ashland, Oregon. She loves swimming in ice-cold water, watching hummingbirds through binoculars, and eating her husband's cooking.

Before becoming a licensed teacher, Robin was a stage manager in regional theaters, and on and off-Broadway.

For thirty years, Robin taught drama to children of all ages in public and private schools. She is the founder of the Pomegranate Preschool for the Arts in Ashland.

Robin's other books include *Pat, Roll, Pull*, (Hachai Publishing), *Liberty Saves the Day* (Colonial Williamsburg Press), and *Whistling for Angela,* a book about adoption (Pajama Press). Her articles have appeared in *Exceptional Parenting Magazine* and *Children's Literature in Education. The Light from My Menorah* will be released by Pajama Press in 2024.

Robin holds an MFAW in Writing for Children from Spalding University, and is represented by Susan Cohen of Writers House.

She is married to actor Anthony Heald. They have two grown children, Dylan and Zoë, and a granddaughter, Amelia Ann.

Alexandra Artigas, a native of Spain, was raised between Europe and South America. Ale has illustrated children's books, educational textbooks and developed characters for almost thirty years, all over the planet. She is passionate about illustrating fun and inspirational projects.

For the last 21 years Ale has been working from her studio in Southern California, and when she is not completely immersed in her illustration projects, you can find her hugging trees, paddle boarding, rock climbing or just enjoying the great outdoors with her beloved family.

You have finished BOOK 3
in the
SAPPHIRE FAMILY SERIES

Book One — *Jackson and Jillian*
Four-year-old twins, Jackson and Jillian, want to brush their teeth by themselves. But when their sister's guinea pig wanders into the bathroom there's a brush with disaster.

Book Two — *Alicia and Annie*
Six-year-old Alicia wants to be a responsible pet owner, but now her pet guinea pig, Annie, is missing. What will Alicia do to make sure Annie stays safe?

Krahn-da Mah-koo!

Additional copies are available through your favorite book dealer, and online or from the publisher (www.robinheald.com). For inquiries, e-mail the author at: robinheald@robinheald.com